Management Consultancy

Problems and Prospects

Ramaswamy Thanu

Printed by Create Space
An Amazon Company

2

Contents

Introduction

Management consultancy is a dignified and noble profession demanding and deploying considerable creativity and innovation. It draws richly on the relevant knowledge from all disciplines ensuring comprehensiveness in approach to problems and solutions. Organizations benefit considerably by drafting the services of consultants who are dedicated to study problems in depth and recommend practical measures for improving performance and profitability. Any organization utilizing resources in any form will benefit from the services of such professionals who are dedicated to help to achieve organizational excellence, reducing costs and utilizing tangible and intangible assets in the most productive manner.

Unfortunately unlike in the case of many other professions there is no statutory compulsion for ensuring the efficiency and productivity in the organizations. The result is resources are not put to the best use. The society loses heavily because of the neglect. and gross mismanagement of the country's resources.

This book is an attempt to highlight some of the problems facing the profession. Some ideas are sown with imparting strength from the wisdom of the ages. It is hoped organizations will consider them seriously.

1. Achilles Heel in the Profession

Management consultancy is one of the noblest professions. It draws knowledge from all disciplines. It is deeply rooted in human creativity and free from shackles of procedures and other hassles normally associated with government organizations evolving solutions to problems. Such creative and innovative nature of the profession helps to create wealth in the country. It helps to reduce waste, reduce costs and improve efficiency. These features serve the cause of humanity by conservation of resources, increasing productivity and improving efficiency saving time and cost to the public. The cost reduction measures originating from management consultancy are not a product of locating and exploiting loopholes in governmental regulations or environment but by designing innovative techniques and measures. But the profession is severely handicapped because of the lack of statutory support. Unlike some other professions where statutory compulsion exists for obtaining the services there is nothing by way of any support demanding compulsion in running the organizations efficiently. The result is organizations are left to manage themselves by adopting practices for keeping ahead of competition in professional or unprofessional ways. The profession is not greed driven. The stringent code of ethics is a healthy sign and it acts as a check on the greed of the members of the profession.

Fees charged by the members are based on parameters within the code of ethics and not on percentage basis either in relation to the volume handled or results attained. Fairness is ensured by charging fees based on effort and time devoted. The core of the matter is that there is no compulsion to be efficient and no compulsion for management audit. It is unfortunate that this profession, though of comparatively recent origin, is not given due recognition by the government taking into account the area for immense benefits at minimum cost Management function is taken lightly and the feeling goes around in many organizations that square pegs can be fitted into round holes. Many are aware that there is a high density cobweb of incompetence in many organizations where efficiency is compromised on populist grounds. But even within the limitations of populist considerations, considerable improvement can be achieved if a degree of compulsion is enforced by way of statutory management audit. This will bring into light unhealthy, harmful management practices in all areas of management. By proper installation of management controls corruption can be minimized .This is easier with the introduction of information technology which helps to reduce the time for mischievous thinking and exercise of discretion in violation of accepted norms and propriety. Till the authorities become aware of the need and act for such a statutory measure, the profession will have to fend for itself relying on its ethics and on the maxim that the sun does not require any certificate to prove its credentials to shine and radiate light. The absence of compulsory management audit acts as the Achilles heel in the profession of management consultants retarding its growth.

2. Corruption Management

Over two thousand five hundred years ago the famous Greek philosopher Aristotle said," Law can control only actions and not motives." He also said. "What the world requires is cleansing of hearts and not of garments". These statements are relevant today. We have been witnessing steady decline in standards of public administration. The growing scale of corruption eats away huge resources of the economy. It is said that in construction industry alone 20% of the funds are washed away by the evil of corruption. This holds true in all other areas of economic and business activity though in varying degrees and proportions.

As management consultants we are interested in ensuring that our knowledge becomes available for conserving resources, using them productively for the benefit of society. The managerial tools of planning and control are inadequate to deal with the problem. We try to quantify the parameters whereas the root of the problem lies in intangibles. We can devise controls taking into account this factor.

.Performance appraisal of employees at all levels including managers should include parameters with yardsticks drawn from our traditional values. It is the value system which triggers or controls motives. If the motives are good the results will be good .The seeds of corruption are sown in the minds of men. So we must attack the problem at that level. Performance appraisal should include parameters to cover the following:

3. Curse of C-Governance

We hear a lot about E- governance these days. But how many have come across C -governance. While the former is governance by adopting electronic means of communication, the latter can be taken to mean governance by corruption. Though no government openly admits this, the fact is that it exists and grows. The result is that the citizens suffer mentally and financially while the officials becoming prosperous. We have some examples to understand how this type of governance works and how sanity and fairness are discounted in favor of dishonesty and duplicity.

Corruption and greed dominate most of the democracies in the world. Even for discharging normal duties, officials who draw salary from the exchequer, resort to extraction of benefits from the recipients of services. This takes the form of cash, gifts, funding personal bills, perquisites, funding admissions, sponsorships etc. The list is exhaustive. The tentacles of C governance spread far and wide and it becomes difficult to pull them out from their strongholds.

Cash is demanded for expediting decisions for favors promised or given. Sometimes promises remain promises even though payments take place. Otherwise service dangles a sword in the form of harassment. So people pay for the service of not harassing. In some cases we find officials accepting cash and gifts amounting to hefty sums for promising the agent or contractor not to harass him, and to overlook delays in the execution of works. These are distinct services rendered by the officials. Perquisites like booking hotel accommodation in five star hotels travel in luxury cars, offer of domestic appliances of all conceivable types, air tickets for travel for family within the country and abroad are examples, which are offshoots of C- governance. These apart, there are novel ways of accepting gratification. These are asking various persons who are the beneficiaries, to sponsor events like admission of children to professional institutions, marriages where each area of activity is assigned to one contractor or agency who will arrange for the supplies but make hush payments in full. Here the ordering official who dispenses the services declares him honest because he says he doesn't touch cash. The beneficiary (recipient) directly makes payments to the institutions and other destinations and thus saves effort, trouble and money for the official.

Violating norms and rules is no problem for these officials. They will twist facts and rules to their advantage when temptations are heavy and backed by hefty money packs. They don't call it a bribe but service charges. Harassment is adopted as a technique for extracting cash and other benefits. For this the provider asks for AHF.This means Anti Harassment Fee. This is considered a service and is liberally approved by the entire officialdom covering all hierarchies irrespective of time and place.

These apart, cuts in purchases and commissions take place. The percentages are set prior to finalizing the deal and the manner and form of payment is determined beforehand. There are also conduits (persons) who will mobilize cash and deliver to the provider. The technique used to benefit the beneficiary client is to disqualify the best supplier by declaring his goods as defective. There are inspection agencies that are specially assigned the job. In one case higher price covering kickbacks was offered for supply of aluminum conductors. The seeker got a higher price. When asked how he managed to get it, he said: "we reduce the length of the cable by 250 meters and this covers more than the loss we incur by way of AHF". The receiver honestly inspects the goods without allowing any one else to examine, at delivery site because he knows it is of short length and he alone can certify it as fit and satisfactory.

In appointments C-governance takes place in several forms. Advance payments and part payments are the normal practice. But there are ingenious chaps who come to know about the names of selected candidates. They have close liaison with the personnel department issuing appointment orders. They promise a share of the booty to them also and ask them to withhold the issue of appointment letters for a definite period. During this gap the official visits the various selected candidates, tells them he will get jobs for them. He collects a lump sum amount in advance. The orders are issued. He wins the confidence of the candidates and gets more clients in future. But when he is unable to oblige them he is honest enough to refund the amount in full. This honest deal is given wide publicity, only to bring more victims into his net.

C- Governance eats away resources otherwise available to the community. Costs of projects go up considerably. In construction it is said 20% of the outlay leaks out through this channel of corruption. Inequity is built into the system. Deserving candidates and persons don't get their due for they have not resorted to measures to ensure sure success. The absence of ethics is the cause for this state of affairs. The receiver and giver have jettisoned all value systems and developed an elastic conscience to justify their actions.

Huge purchase, large deals involving millions of dollars bring windfalls to champions of C governance. The collections prior to elections for party funding imply this principle by extending invitations to liberally fill deep pockets for receiving cash.

The funniest thing is that the enforcing agency, whose job is to prevent and detect such types of C-governance official, also falls a victim and benefit by huge inflow of funds and perquisites. There are many in the hierarchy and chain to share the spoils. Examples are many. But with one more we conclude this topic. There are entry points at the borders of states. The vehicles have to produce valid documents for entry. The officials who conduct the checking have an eagle's eye to detect where the client has placed a hefty cover in a designated corner of the shed he is using for official work. In the evening a huge amount accumulates and according to an agreed formula the spoils are shared. Many of them have palatial buildings with all gadgets and amenities, luxury cars and facilities for children to study in the best of professional institutions. All these are the blessings of C- Governance. This is pampered, promoted and perpetuated by the government for all benefit .The only loser and the aggrieved individual is the honest law-aiding citizen. He can only cry for E- governance and Good- governance. But how can he destroy C- governance. Elections at frequent intervals only bring this evil back in greater strength and vigor for all want it badly. We all long for a day when C-government will be wiped out in the interest of sound administration and equity for all citizens.

4. Conference on Corruption

A Police Chief felt corruption was rampant in his department. This malady has been a source of headache for him. He received several complaints from the public. Finally he decided to convene a conference on corruption obviously to assess the extent of the malady and to find remedies. This required participation of all senior officials above the rank of Police Inspectors. Accordingly conference was held with attendance of over 45 officials.

The Chief explained briefly the purpose of the conference and sought the cooperation of the members in devising ways and means of eliminating corruption in the department. He gave a bit of his mind to those present. In particular he had a dig at officials who had a high propensity for corruption. At the same time he asked them to be fearless in expressing their views and comments.

The conference began.

Chief:" I am shocked to hear complaints about corruption in the police force. This is very bad for the reputation of the department. You have to take immediate steps to eliminate this evil. We must wipe off corruption".

There was total silence. Then a voice came from the

eastern side of the table. One senior official, SNK, stood up and expressed his views fearlessly.

SNK: "Sir, what you say was true till now. Today we find we are in a better position."

Chief: "Why? What is the wonderful development?"

SNK:" Sir: We are not as corrupt as we were before. The scope for corruption is much less now".

Chief: "How do you say that? The public is enraged over a recent incident in which a Police Inspector took bribe for closing his eyes to a traffic offence."

SNK: "Sir, I said it on behalf of the police department. In Traffic there is scope. Daily each member of staff takes home at least 400 bucks. The efficiency of the department is rated based on the collection they make. In fact we would welcome occasional postings by rotation there. That department is a high milk-yielding cow.

Chief:" I understand your anxiety to be part of that department. But there are complaints from public about Traffic also.

SNK: "True Sir. Complaints will always remain, as long the human beings exist. But we have to be practical."
Chief:" Are you teaching me practicality?"
SNK: "No Sir, I am only mentioning the fact. We have a moderately large family to support. They have several needs. They see their peers living in high style. Should we not give them some semblance of it?
Chief: "I very well understand and appreciate that. I am prepared to take a lenient view. Now I want you to come to the point you originally made. That is regarding the lack of scope for corruption. I don't agree. I shall tell you an anecdote".

"There was a King. He had a stable with 50 horses. One day an ordinary citizen by name RST remarked that a government job brings large patronage and of course lot of money. Even with a salary of 1 buck a month you can earn 1000 bucks in a year. He said this in public and this news reached the ears of the King. The deeply annoyed King sent for the person and asked him about the truth of the statement. First he denied having made any such statement. Finally he admitted. He extolled the virtues of government job even if it carried a very low salary. The King cornered him with the statement whether even with a salary of 1 buck per month he would earn 1000 bucks in a year. The man admitted and said 'yes'."

The King gave him a stern warning and said: " Now I give you a job on 1-buck salary. You must produce 1000 bucks in a year in your account. I give you a job. You will assume full charge of horses in the royal stable on a salary of 1-buck per month. You will have to show me a fat bank balance at the end of the year".

RST took charge of the new assignment. He visited the stable. But before taking up the new job he laid down a condition before the special officer JAN in charge of horses. This official reported direct to the King on matters relating to horses and the feed for the animals.

RST: "Sir, I wish to submit one thing before you. The King has given me a very heavy responsibility and I have to discharge my duties faithfully. For this I need a designation, a portable weighing balance and stationery"

. JAN did not know the implications of this. He readily agreed. The equipments were given and he designated RST as Horse Dung Superintendent. (HDS). The designation was communicated to all. HDS took to his job with all seriousness"

He went round and gave each horse an identification code, a card in which the horseman was asked to enter daily the details of feed given, weight, and the output of dung. The data were recorded daily and he examined them. For the first three days there was no serious discrepancy in the quantities of inputs and outputs. Form the fourth day onwards the output weighed considerably less compared to the earlier figures. He identified all such cases and called for explanation from the horsemen."

"In fact they had committed minor pilferage of feed by diverting part of it home. When he grilled them they admitted. All agreed to give him 1 buck per day for 25 days a month. Thus each horseman gave 25 bucks to the HDS every month. In a year the amount thus collected came to 300 bucks per horse. The King remembered the date on which his bank account was to banish. He called for the account book. He was surprised to find the entries revealing a fat figure including interest. This exceeded 15000 rupees. The King saluted HDS for his ingenuity and regularized his appointment on a higher salary."

Chief: "Do you know why I am telling this story? It is because I want to point out the great scope for corruption in fields unheard of and where the possibilities were thought to be nil. So SNK, don't say there is less scope. I don't want you to excel the HDS in generating private revenue. But do it discreetly so that you can earmark a portion for us too. In our heart of hearts we want people like you who will siphon off funds carefully and to benefit large number of officials apart from you."

SNK: "Sir, I am an honest person. I said this only as an example. I will not touch cash by hand. I will ask my wife or friend to do the collection so that my name does not figure anywhere".

Chief: That is a good idea. Any way gets results. That is all what I want. In corruption there is one thing. We are getting something for a service we give to the beneficiary. You don't lose anything. Beneficiary doesn't lose. The HDS as well as the horsemen got their quota of loot from the quantity allotted to them. The reduced intake did not harm the horse in any way. That was because all these quantities were inflated. This is a transaction where all entities benefit and there is collective happiness".

"Is there anybody here who would like to give his views or comments?"

TJJ: "Sir I have one question. You have pointed out the scope where ingenuity is high. But we have to get the participation of all officials in the department who form various links in the chain. They have to be involved. So they should also benefit. For this I suggest decentralization of functions .You can take decisions at the district level. When powers are decentralized corruption also is decentralized. It will be a landmark in simplifying administrative procedures".

The Chief welcomed this idea.

He said: "For this purpose a special committee would be

constituted. This would go into the merits of the case for decentralization. We should study the implications before we do anything. In order to protect and safeguard our interest I nominate SNK to the committee as Chairman. Let us all swear by corruption and push it under the carpet. The conference was over.

S

5. Ancient Wisdom and Consulting

This chapter deals with a vital area, which has been perhaps left out by the management consultancy profession. This could bring substantial benefits to organizations and ultimately to humanity in terms of wealth, happiness and sustainability of resources. Being a noble profession, management consultancy welcomes knowledge from all disciplines and areas of knowledge for solution of managerial problems. It has benefited considerably by opening its doors to welcome knowledge from many areas. It has contributed to the enrichment of the management profession by formulating approaches having wide applications.

However, it is sad to note that the most promising source of strength for the profession to benefit organizations and humanity has not been given adequate importance. The purpose of this series of articles is to bring out the quintessence of the knowledge, -vital for value creation, innovation and knowledge management.

Value creation is creating value by applying knowledge available to us in any area of human activity with a management orientation. This is to bring about productive and useful results in organizations benefiting several people. . Innovation is bringing out something new but which can revolutionize our ways of living. Knowledge management is managing or making use of available knowledge for attaining definite objectives. Management consultancy has the objective of designing and applying concepts, tools and techniques for the improved performance of organizations. This has to be consistent with ethics and resource availability.

Let us consider for a while what is happening to value creation? Here it is worthwhile raising a few questions. Are we creating value always to attain the maximum potential? In terms of monetary and production value we are adding to value. But in terms of consumer satisfaction, happiness and sustainability of resources are we adding value? Are we not producing low priority goods and services on the pretext of economic growth? In reality there is knowledge explosion but not always in the right direction. We all ideally aim that this knowledge should benefit a vast majority of people. Knowledge is not required for knowledge sake. It should be sustainable knowledge. It should be such that its growth has to be only to the extent ethics support it. Otherwise that knowledge becomes harmful or redundant.

In effect a small section of people benefit substantially and the others get marginal benefit. It is this distorted knowledge management that restricts the field of operations of management consultancy confining it to industry and organizations.

6. Systems Approach

We talk about systems approach for solving problems. This envisages a total approach to problem solving using relevant knowledge from all disciplines considering the system and subsystems. But have we seriously tried to use relevant valuable knowledge from spirituality-based sources, which constitute a subsystem of knowledge? These sources originate from ancient scriptures of wisdom, which greatly emphasize human excellence. They focus on the individual. We know human resources are very important. We all appreciate the role of motivation in achieving performance. But do we recognize the power within man to excel in performance and how this could be tapped and realized in terms of potential. This is an omission needing immediate attention and correction.

This vital knowledge is available to us for thousands of years. Great sages of vision, who had only the good of humanity in mind, evolved this. There is very little evidence of the quintessence of our ancient wisdom being used by the management consultancy profession in an organized manner.

It is the spirit within man, which makes living possible and in whose presence alone all human action and achievement are possible. It is the divinity that really illumines the functioning of the body. It imparts strength to men and managers if they realize its presence and are attached to it. The thought that one is the spirit gives strength and this is a vital force, which motivates. It helps to view the body as an instrument of action. It propels one to excel in performance without craving for rewards.

The inspiration one gets from such a faith is tremendous. This created many leaders in India and abroad. They shook the world with their power of thoughts and actions. Such men had a conceptual approach not confined to any organization but to the whole country and even beyond. It is this approach that gave them a vision and dynamism to achieve human excellence. They were real leaders worthy of emulation.

Mahatma Gandhi was an example. He conceived India as one integrated whole. He was highly motivated. He had a supra ordinary goal. He lived and worked with a sense of fulfillment without expecting anything except the welfare of his countrymen. If management consultancy imparts this strength to leadership development we will have an increasing number of highly productive and motivated leaders. This will occur not only in industrial and business organizations but in other fields of national importance also. Their contribution will be undoubtedly positive, productive and far-reaching. Same is the case with managers and entrepreneurs. They will be charged with the power of dynamism to make their contribution more effective and substantial.

7. Scriptures and Wisdom

The insights into our ancient scriptures reveal genuine wisdom, which if applied will definitely help the profession to be more effective. The offshoots of such a value creating philosophy will be of a high order. Such a list will cover time management, motivation, functional specialization, human relations, conflict elimination, ethics oriented strategy, energy conservation, cost reduction, waste elimination, human excellence etc. The philosophy definitely adds to value. It ensures better knowledge management.

The conceptual skills are embedded in works of ancient wisdom. We apply them to the enterprise and that skill becomes important for the CEO. When one develops a universal mind the perspective of the CEO changes. He broadens his vision and is able to ensure and discharge his social responsibilities, which are cared for spontaneously. There will be a natural built in mechanism for resolving conflicts in organizations because the degree of understanding will be great.

Let us consider some areas where the ancient wisdom rooted in spirituality is of help to us. It clearly emphasizes the importance of goal setting for the individual. Management also stresses this whether it is an organization or a department. Individual goals crystallized will be tuned to the organization's goal and management by objectives will be better realized. The merit here is something unique in that such objectives and actions are based on ethics.

Management training is considered an important aspect of executive and organization development. This is preparing the executive for higher responsibilities. Ancient wisdom does this in a more effective way. It lays down discipline-Spartan discipline, through techniques like yoga to tune the body and health, and meditation to tune the mind for concentration. It stresses the role of positive thinking for purifying thoughts facilitating right decisions and judgment. It creates leadership models.

The kings and leaders of the past were role models and they set examples of good administration. Case studies for leadership development, duties and responsibilities and interpersonal relations, from the great epics like Ramayana and Mahabharata help to improve leadership training.

Management lays stress on training, which is equipping oneself for executive position. Ancient wisdom emphasizes equipping oneself with qualities for learning and grasping. It stipulated proper diets and physical exercise for men of action to withstand strain. Yoga is considered to be a very effective technique. It is effectively equipping oneself unlike the holiday approach of the modern executive. We applaud modern expressions like executive lunch but fail to understand the prevalence of better diet packages for men thousands of years ago.

8. Applications

Ancient wisdom places emphasis on hard work, which is a form of penance. Thus maximum energy is conserved and not frittered away. The discipline at the student stage called brahmacharya is intended to benefit oneself and humanity. In that stage faith, competence and discipline are developed. These are vital for success in any field of human endeavour.

Motivation is built into the individual for he is given a supra ordinary goal of love towards all. This widens his horizon of thinking. He is in a better position to understand human behavior and resolve conflicts.

Time management is effectively advocated by emphasis on living in the present. The past is gone and there is no point in brooding over the events and mistakes of the past. Today's present becomes tomorrow's past. The future is not in our hands and is full of uncertainty. But the present is with us and is within our control. The future of today becomes present of tomorrow. So there is only present. If the present is well utilized the future is taken care of. Preoccupations of the past are not allowed to influence the present. Similarly anxieties over the future are not allowed to affect performance in the present. This ensures maximum efficiency and productivity. The entire energy is available for current use.

Developing a universal mind develops a total approach and thus conceptual skill. The body, mind and intellect are only instruments of action. By properly tuning them according to the ways advocated in the scriptures the efficiency of each will be fully achieved and sound decisions ensured. This is understood through the beautiful concept of self-management, which enables one to attain human excellence. This can be further refined as a technique of management training for executive excellence. This will also conserve energy and increase productivity in areas where goals are set.

Living a moderate way of life and changed life style will reduce down time caused by illness and diseases. Emphasis on simple ways of living will brings down costs of inputs. This ensures cost control and elimination of waste.

The value system with emphasis on achieving the objective within the framework of basic ethics is a wonderful gift of ancient wisdom. It says righteousness is the basis of all actions Acquiring wealth should be conditioned by righteousness, i.e., only that wealth, which fulfils the criterion of righteousness, should be attempted. This applies to fulfilling other desires also. When everything is rooted in righteousness corruption and greed will not raise their heads or will be minimal. In management training we have to emphasize this aspect of the basis of wealth creation subject to righteousness.

All executive actions should be based on righteousness. Each profession with reference to their respective sphere can define what constitutes this virtue. Management consultancy can also do. We have been vaguely talking about business ethics and code of conduct but that is not enough. Consultants deal with several organizations of differing background and culture. With reference to each organization righteousness can be expounded and advice given.

9. Self Management

The management consultancy profession should focus on cooperation than competition. The former avoids waste and saves resources whereas the latter promotes waste and boosts up costs. Globally this principle of cooperation in lieu of competition has been accepted. That is why we have organizations like the WTO, EEC to ensure smooth economic transactions between countries.

It is beneficial to focus on self-management to promote human excellence, which is one of the most important objectives of management consultancy. The focus on training the body, mind and intellect for maintaining health, fitness, discipline, stress free existence and clear thinking for right decisions is ensured.

In all areas of consultancy the basic anchor should be righteousness. Wealth creation and acquisition should be based on this principle. This will remove greed and corrupt tendencies in organizations. It is beneficial to include among objectives of organizations the following important one- to create wealth subject to the condition that such process is firmly rooted in righteousness. The same approach is applicable to satisfying consumer desires. The availability of harmful goods and services should be restricted and gradually withdrawn.

Management consultancy is a noble profession. It can act as a catalyst to effect significant changes in standards of living and economic progress with sustainability. It should give emphasis on creating wealth in sectors where the poor people will largely benefit so that poverty will be eliminated over a period of time. All actions should be based on righteousness, i.e., fairness and transparency in dealings. Training programs should offer this as the thrust area. If this fundamental aspect is ignored the economic system will operate to the common detriment. The activities of the organization and society should be value driven and not greed driven.

This may appear to be a utopian philosophy of management. But we have to aim high and keep the ideal up and not pull it down in the name of practicality. If we do so then we are elevating the status of a thief to that of an effective, efficient and most successful manager. This is because he does not use any resources of his own to attain his objectives of stealing. Even the tools he uses are stolen. The access to concepts and methods for human excellence implied and advocated in the works of ancient wisdom confers several benefits on consultants. The Bhagavad-Gita gives us all essential knowledge for human excellence. It ensures sustainability in several areas like environment, resources exploitation, technology etc. At the individual level whether it is employee or CEO it can definitely bring results. These could be in terms of conservation of energy, resources, industrial peace, and balanced infrastructure and overall growth of the economy. Such growth will ensure equity, fairness and life balance.

Any individual who is trained with armor of spirituality will be an asset to society. He will not steal. Nor will he create law and order problems. He will enjoy life and make others happy. He will let others live happily. This is true whether he is a CEO or employee or a citizen. It is hoped the future generations of management consultants will seriously dive deep to the springs of ancient wisdom. It is our prayer that they draw as much as possible, modify and perfect them. It is our fervent hope that they will graft them into the consultancy profession so that organizations and societies benefit substantially.

10 .21st Century Vision

This chapter seeks to identify the basic hurdle of the consultancy profession to ensure effectiveness and results in the age of E Governance for resource utilization and poverty alleviation. It refers to C governance directly and indirectly promoting corporate frauds and the need for reducing political content in decision-making globally. It lays stress on imparting ethics and value systems in management enlarging the scope of the consultancy profession in framing solutions for the twin problems of corruption and poverty alleviation richly drawing from the treasure of ancient wisdom.

These days we talk about E Governance, which has many laudable objectives and beneficial results. Procedures have been simplified considerably. The common man has experienced most of the benefits as in the case of railway reservations. But what actually happens in many cases of administration and management is C Governance. This simply stated is Corruption in Governance. They block the smooth flow of benefits and convenience to the common man. Corrupt practices influence decision-making particularly involving huge financial outlays. Everywhere expectations grow tall and fast but are not fulfilled. The enormous intangible resource within man, the mind and intellect, is rarely tapped and full potential realized for solving problems.

We come across cases of political corruption through the misuse by government officials of powers and the governmental machinery for illegal personal enrichment. All forms of government are susceptible to play the game of political corruption. Forms of corruption vary. But they include bribery, extortion, nepotism, patronage, graft, and embezzlement. This creates great social injustice particularly to the poor sections of the population. In some countries corruption is widespread that it occurs when ordinary business enterprises or citizens interact with government officials. The terminus of political corruption is a kleptocracy, literally 'rule by thieves'.

Corruption poses a serious development challenge. It undermines good governance by subverting formal processes. Its presence in elections and in legislative bodies reduces accountability and distorts representation in policy making. Corruption in the judiciary compromises the rule of law and that in public administration results in the unfair provision of services. It corrodes and erodes the institutional capacity of government as procedures are disregarded and resources siphoned off.

It undermines economic development by causing all round distortions and inefficiency spreading its tentacles all over the country. In the private sector, corruption jacks up the cost of business through the price of illegal payments, the management fee of negotiating with officials. Though some people observe that corruption reduces costs by eliminating red tape, the availability of bribes induces officials to devise ingeniously new rules and delays.

While corruption inflates the cost of business, it also distorts the playing field, shielding firms with connections from competition and thereby sustaining inefficient firms. Cases are not rare where firms supplying first quality products and services are disqualified in favor of those who are substandard because they could pay off huge amounts as bribes.

It also brings economic distortions in the public sector by diverting public investment into capital projects where bribes and kickbacks are plentiful. Officials dexterously manipulate and increase the technical complexity of public sector projects to conceal or facilitate such dealings.

Corruption also lowers compliance with construction, environmental, or other regulations, reduces the quality of government services and infrastructure, and increases budgetary pressures on government. Siphoning of resources and the resultant wastage thwart the main objectives of good governance. Such compliance brings forth the collapse of building structures soon after they are inaugurated with great fan fare and publicity. National poverty remains without significant change.

Economists profess that one important factor behind the differing economic development in Africa and Asia is that in the former, corruption has primarily taken the garb of rent extraction with the generated financial capital invested overseas rather than at home. Corrupt administrations in Asia have often taken a cut on everything requiring bribes, though provided more of the conditions for development, through infrastructure investment, law and order, etc.

Management consultancy, according to one definition, is: 'the creation of value for organizations, through the application of knowledge, techniques and assets, to improve performance. This is achieved through the rendering of objective advice and/or the implementation of business solutions.' Management consultants are invited into organizations to provide an objective analysis, wider expertise and independent specialist skills. They are primarily concerned with initiating and implementing organizational, behavioral and technological changes.

World economic progress, in general, during the last decade has been remarkable. Productivity and employment have increased in many fields and industrial growth has been over 9% in some countries. Globalization has brought easy and abundant availability of goods and services in the country. Some countries have moved far away from a state when gold movements took place for settling international obligations to a state where they have foreign exchange reserves of over $300 billion. The stock markets are booming with activity and massive inflow of investment from abroad takes place. But C governance also gets a boost eating away part of the resources earmarked for development.

The consultant's role and effectiveness is affected by the predominance of C-governance in all areas of activity. Sometimes client organization wants the consultant to give reports defending the decision already taken or to give a report as per the parameters set by the client, against facts, professional integrity and ethics. This prevents level playing field for those who believe in fair business practices. Thus the best of expertise on the assignment becomes non-usable. C- Governance has elevated bribing to the status of a result oriented management technique. This is particularly true in marketing. Cases are not rare where consultants are sought to do stealthily industrial espionage even by large companies. There are also cases where decisions are hurriedly taken by organizations and consultants are asked to support them by tutored and structured studies, which are based on manipulated facts. Wastage of resource arises on account of C- governance i.e. governmental activity driven by corruption and greed. This creates a chain reaction bringing the evil effects of corruption all through the hierarchy down to the lowest level. Apart from causing depletion of resources, this promotes wide disparity in incomes and growth. C-Governance and greed of the officialdom choke decision-making and create obstacles in the way of economic progress though it is said to act as an expediting process.

The democratic system as it functions today in some countries does not permit penetration of professionalism in politics with the most appropriate skills. It is devoid of ethics. Countries like Singapore where the politicians occupying ministerial posts are high caliber professionals are few. The exclusion of politicians from the network of developing core competence for ruling the country and managing the economy distorts the system. Exceptions are rare.

This takes us to the question of widening the scope of consultancy services and area of responsibilities. Consultants are concerned with conservation and optimum utilization of resources. Does the consultancy profession have any responsibility for devising ways and means of improving performance in developing core competence and national progress? Of all human resources leadership is the most important. This is the core resource.

The seeds of C- governance are sown in the minds of politicians. They are nurtured by the flush of funds originating through corrupt means of party funding which is not subject to audit and scrutiny in some countries. This encourages a chain of hierarchies, creating powerful and unbreakable links with officials and donors who disrupt the sound management of the economy. The gravitational pull of such negative leadership downwards slows down progress and performance.

While there are hundreds of types of audit which have been made statutory, there is no statutory management audit. There is no compulsion to be efficient. It is the neglect of one of the most important areas, which could ensure productive utilization of resources for progress, and its cumulative effect that has created a huge overburden of versatile incompetence in the core sectors. Inadequacies in professional skills at the top layers of the government and the dominance of vested interests, act as an insulated shield preventing the penetration of most effective managerial tools.

Luckily the IT industry is comparatively free from the menace of political interference. Politicians do not tamper with it because many are not familiar with the complexity of the industry. Further Companies, which have achieved tremendous growth and success, attribute their achievement due to their philosophy of being value driven and not greed driven. The management of such companies has been able to resist pressures from the government officials to dilute the standard of ethics in dealings. They become victims of C- governance.

Can consultants in general and management consultancy in particular effectively help to tackle the twin evil of C Governance and poverty? Is there any set of effective tools they can design and adopt? If so how can it be done and how soon. Can this be made as part of the vision for the 21st century for all countries? These questions take us to the objective of widening the scope of consultancy services. The emphasis is to demolish the pillars of C governance and promote E Governance, which has brought benefits to the common man with prospects of greater benefits and convenience.

Management welcomes knowledge from all disciplines. It believes in an inter-disciplinary approach. It upholds the systems approach for solving problems. It has widely applied the systems approach for solving problems in industry. In the area of corruption and poverty elimination too there are vital subsystems. They remain outside the system and disrupt the fulfillment of the objective of economic growth with equity and social harmony. These include the politicians, the legislature and the judiciary.

One important area of knowledge demanding close and immediate attention is application of ethics in governmental administration. Such ethics derive strength from spirituality. In fact contrary to popular belief this is totally secular and universally beneficial. This has recently gained acceptance in western countries as a tool of managerial effectiveness. Countries and organizations where officials take orders from a situation and not from individuals have benefited from using such tools.

Concepts like Dharmic Management have surfaced and found greater acceptance. Real values of life do contain potential for improving the quality of human resource, which commands other resources. India's rich heritage and wisdom provide ample evidence of this potential. There is no need to feel shy about using such beneficial tools and management consultants can freely make use of them.

Twenty first century is going to be the century fusing economic progress with spiritual strength. It augurs well for the world economy. Countries with spiritual strength hold the beacon of hope and leadership for world development. Wisdom and the heritage of the past dating back to thousands of years teach us the art of man making. This is the unique strength India has, which others are yet to acquire. If man is developed to attain excellence, the family, society, nation, country and the whole world will attain better growth and harmony.

So the most important aspect of human development is to develop man to attain his maximum potential. His assets are the body, mind and intellect the three pillars on which his excellence is built. Intellect can be trained to develop positive thinking ensuring right decisions. The mind can be developed to imbibe values, which will benefit humanity. The body can be kept healthy so that work can be done at peak efficiency with little down time.

While developing all these aspects the unseen resource of spiritual strength - that is belief in the spirit behind the three faculties, which makes them function, is to be respected and relied upon. We may call it life, energy or consciousness. Any work in any field of activity if done with this vision will bring better results. It will make any professional a better professional in his field. It will be done with a sense of dedication. Great men and leaders who made tremendous contribution to the country were those who had strengths deeply rooted in spirituality. They were motivated to excel in their performance through a sense of fulfillment and they acted far beyond enriching themselves. Conceptual skill was imbedded in them and they could visualize the country as one integrated whole. They practiced sustainability by respecting environmental forces. We also know the most essential things in life; air, water, space and fire are free. Without them life will be extinct. But we often forget how they came to be provided and what is the force, which sustains them. It is the realization of this truth that takes us to see and respect the spirit behind all these free resources, which are essentials and for which no monetary value can be assigned or will be adequate.

Optimum utilization of resources implies prevention of wastage. Breakdown of law and order is a major source of such loss. How can consultants produce maximum results in terms of national benefits? What is the most valuable tool for the consultant? Are we sincerely and steadily striving for human excellence in all areas of activity? The existing tools, techniques and concepts are inadequate. This is seen from the prevalence of C Governance and corporate frauds, which globally exist.

Some universities in Western countries are giving importance to introducing values and spiritual orientation to management practices. Consultants will benefit if they realize the relevance and strength of the core values that substantially help to attain human excellence. Is it enough if they remain in a sense of complacency entertaining the belief that the limitations cannot be overcome and they have to accept and live with them?

Ancient times witnessed rulers and leaders who were men of integrity, vision and concern for the people's prosperity with harmony. They set examples of honest living and strong concern for the people. Unfortunately there is no mechanism by which the professional integrity and honesty of political leaders is improved .Law can control only actions but not motives. Very little is done for promoting the role of character in economic development and in nation building. Character springs forth from a value system.

Just like the role of top management in ensuring good results for business organizations, political leaders have to ensure good results in ensuring good governance. This is possible only if they are well equipped. An attempt to equip them by fits and starts merely through seminars and conferences will not yield lasting results.

Consultants will benefit by undertaking research for improving the productivity of political leaders who have to be development oriented. They have to promote development leadership. For funding programs of leadership development financing by government or by large business houses can be explored.

The scope of activity of the consultants should include in-depth study of political organizations, their funding, managerial practices, weaknesses and steps to strengthen them with clear objectives in tune with the country's constitution. They are in a better position to study in depth, examine facts objectively and present findings fearlessly.

The only remedy for arresting C governance is to impart a value system along with other tools and techniques of management. It is not wise to equate serendipity with genius. Political leaders, who have a clean record of miserable failure in their chosen career fields, at times have shown unbelievably good results in totally different areas. This has been a subject of study and appreciation by management institutes and B schools abroad. This is laudable. But the results have to be consistent and sustained.

The factors governing success in such cases should be identified, analyzed, and used as guidance for transplanting elsewhere. If consultants can identify the causes for poor performance with a view to improve and bring out the results in public they can have an impact on the quality of governance marking a beginning of the process of demolition of the fortress of C Governance .

A well designed management control system can bring substantial improvement to minimize the impact of C governance. This facilitates early detection of fraudulent practices. This is all the more easy when real time computerized control systems are possible. Human excellence should be the goal of all organizations. Only if the top political layers in government and administration have the will to implement measures to achieve excellence, beneficial results will percolate and prevail in all organizations and hierarchies.

The management consultant has to accept a major role in national planning and reconstruction. Planning is concerned with utilizing resources most productively. The consultant's job is to ensure this by evolving tools and techniques, which include motivating men. India's ancient heritage upholds the cause of humanity. The concepts and principles of administration and human conduct framed thousands of years ago had that end in view. They hold good even now.

The value system definitely provides answers to many problems of administration and human relationships. They seek to ensure good conduct, fairness and equity in administration and healthy human relationships. Here quantitative and other techniques fail. We have to develop an open mind to be convinced about their worth, relevance and applicability.

We don't have to search for new tools. Actually we have only to discover the essential and most productive tools from India's ancient heritage without being prejudiced. Indian value system is the greatest global asset. It is the springboard for character formation and ultimately human destiny. This is clear from the following verse.

Sow a thought and reap an idea,
Sow an idea and reap an act,
Sow an act and reap a character
Sow a character and reap a destiny.

Management consultancy needs a wider definition to include within its ambit of operations studying the value system imbedded in our heritage and scriptures. We have to dig out and apply those with modification, convert them into productive tools to suit present day conditions. These are in the areas of time management, motivation, communications, organizational behavior, avoidance of conflict, human welfare, sustainable living standards, life balance, conservation of resources and environment.

A systems approach incorporating the value system for demolishing C Governance in organizations- political, social and economic will be productive of results. This will ensure right leadership, for thrust will be given using training methods to promote development leadership. The profession of management consultants has to go beyond corporate governance and corporate leadership. It should focus on developing leaders for political excellence.

It is essential for the healthy and sustained growth of the economy and for improving the standard of living of the poorer sections of the population that the tool of self-management techniques is given wide application by consultants. India's rich heritage with an ocean of sacred literature contains enough material for unearthing tools and concepts of relevance to modern conditions and times.

The exclusion of this factor as a subsystem for problem solving has been the cause of retrogression and growth of

C governance. This lapse has resulted in system failure and retarded national progress, making it lopsided. Often, there is no national perspective and this lack of conceptual skill on the part of those running the government has resulted in more efforts and time being devoted for resolving conflicts and clash of interests.

Consultants have to widen their vision beyond the present restricted area of industry and business. Poverty elimination is an important area where they have to evolve new tools. Education is another area. Similarly with social harmony they have to play a role. They have to devise tools for improvements in law and order and for effective functioning of the judiciary within the constitutional provisions. Dogmas and conventional tools are becoming obsolete. We should not give a stone when one wants bread.

Consultants will do well to widen the horizon of thinking and evolve tools and techniques to tackle the problem of C governance and poverty alleviation. The concepts of motivational economics and development leadership are helpful for this. This approach has to go parallel with efforts at E governance.

While it is laudable to have billionaires among the middle class, it is also necessary in the interests of stability and harmony in society; those below the poverty level are lifted up economically. Those who manage the national economy, the highest levels in the government need to have more of professional content in their decision making. The political content has to be minimized. It is this political content, of high dosage, which brings in its train all vices. It introduces unfair and unethical practices feeding the machine of C Governance causing it to spread its tentacles far and wide.

This calls for new consultancy objectives. These have to go beyond corporations and organizations and include political organizations particularly in the area of development leadership. The built in hurdles for social harmony and progress have to be identified, pointed out, studied and remedial measures recommended. Management consultants being a free and independent body can do this in the national interest.

Democracy does not mean willful atrophy of human faculty and potential. We should not allow things to drift. The consultants are very much concerned about their reputation to act as catalysts to produce desirable and beneficial results to their client organizations. Clients should get decisive results to benefit the organization, all employees and shareholders. The society needs to benefit by cost effective recommendations and results flowing from implementation. Policy makers have to make changes in polices to permit consultants to choose any area for study where social benefits will be considerable and in the national interest.

Statutory management audit of organizations will definitely help. This is not to develop the consultant but to benefit the nation by plugging leakages in the system of resource utilization. Academics and professionals can evolve new areas of research, which include a reliable systems approach to solution of national problems bringing in its fold the world of waste generation and willful resource annihilation.

The conventional tools apart, tools from ancient wisdom of this land can be taken and developed. This will strengthen the declaration of management that it welcomes knowledge from all disciplines and the discipline of ethics and spirituality will be brought within its fold. This will definitely be a value addition to the professional knowledge.

E governance could be supplemented and facilitated by management concepts and tools with high ethical and spiritual content to attain human excellence and resource utilization. Such concepts are readily available in our scriptures like Bhagavad-Gita On-line real time information will help to expedite the decision making process and reduce the opportunity for champions of C governance to exploit the delays converting them into money and benefits. Other measures desirable are:

Persuading national leaders to adopt management tools, which will increase the professional content in their decisions and ensure social harmony and progress? Bringing out research findings of studies on benefits and havoc caused by good/poor leadership and recommend remedial measures seeking funds from business houses if not provided by the government.

- The measures deserving serious consideration are:
- Including management consultants forming units for specialized study and research on social harmony, law and order

Development leadership forming a National Social Security Fund to benefit the poor

Substituting C governance by E governance

imparting professional training for political leaders
And

Linking spirituality and management to form the base for individual and national character formation and human excellence.

Politicians have to be professionals. They should be equipped with the concepts, knowledge, and tools including values to discharge their responsibilities to the people. Value and ethics do have a vital role in attaining human excellence, motivating the followers and conserving resources. Democracy does not advocate wanton wastage of resources by inaction and core incompetence. It does not envisage a form of government by human drainpipes. It is time to draft mature competent selective politicians as part of the consultancy profession to interact and to make them realize what professionals can do for the country.

Management consultancy should look beyond business and industry. Ethics and character come from spiritual outlook and they play a vital role in harmonious, sure and sustained economic development. This constitutes the core resource development strategy. It is developing the individual in whatever capacity he is, using the value based concepts, techniques and tools drawn from our ancient wisdom realizing the potential of the mind, body and intellect. It will help to achieve better life balance and harmony.

21st century is destined to be the century of spirituality, which can impart great strength and purpose to human endeavour. In this area India has a great role to play and contribute to world prosperity. It has demonstrated this with the effulgence of its native intelligence and brainpower. It suits the genius of India. Its heritage depicts the finest of values systems, principles of social harmony and motivation to view performance as a source of self-fulfillment.

The heritage if rightly understood and assimilated, offers solutions to all problems of mankind. It is a question of bringing a vast number of people within its disciplined approach. The tools of mind control and positive thinking ensure productivity and equity. It helps to conserve the environment. Leadership quality will considerably improve to turn many politicians into statesmen.

Mankind owes so much to India's ancient wisdom. Works of wisdom like the Bhagavad-Gita contain teachings many of which have management implications particularly in the area of human excellence. There is nothing higher than the Gita as a source of motivation and excellence for nation building and leadership development. Only men of character and vision deeply rooted in sound management principles and ancient wisdom can make a nation culturally and economically strong. This is the objective of self-management.

Any activity turns more productive if spiritual strength is imparted. Management and spirituality are creative pursuits and both stress on optimum resource utilization. While the former deals with external resources the latter develops internal faculties of man.

Our environmentalists discovered the need for conservation of natural wealth only recently whereas India's ancient sages discovered and propagated this concept thousands of years ago. The mind is said to be a $10 billion gift. We must stretch our minds to the farthest limit. This is an extension of the management concept of thinking big.

Conserving our energy and cultivating positive values will greatly help the cause of management. It is the purifier, which will help to liquidate all evil tendencies in the mind. There will be no source of disturbance and one can attain great freedom from stress, which is a malady of the modern executive.

Spiritual strength is the greatest asset of any individual and nation. A manager benefits considerably and attains Total Quality Management by developing and holding on to it. Thus we achieve a better quality of life. It is worth remembering the old saying "Better a moment of glow than a lifetime of smoke".

Management consultancy will grow by leaps and bounds and gain a lot if it brings spirituality in its fold as part of a systems approach to efficient value based and result oriented management. It is worthwhile to remember the formula practiced by the Japanese management i.e., Faith + Discipline + Hard work = Success. This if faithfully followed and with ethics and spiritual strength success will be guaranteed.

When conventional concepts, tools and techniques fail or are found too inadequate, the value system rightly tapped and utilized, will bring success.

Let us hope such an approach and a success formula will go global and will be accepted in the near future.

In the Twenty-first century we have achieved amazing progress materially in raising the standard of living of the people in general. There has been tremendous knowledge explosion and the knowledge industry is growing rapidly. The world has shrunk in terms of distances and become a village with vast connectivity thanks to the Internet and jet travel. Science and technology are advancing at tremendous speed. There is increase in GDP of most countries. Medical science has advanced and longevity of man has increased. More countries are joining the list of developed countries. Opportunities for material advancement are increasing. But can we say with certainty we have used our knowledge to improve the quality of life of man?

Have we attained the quality of life warranted by the rate and quantum of progress we have achieved? The ingredients of this are good health, positive thinking, improvement in character; compassion for others; inherent tendency and urge to help others, capacity to do one's allotted duty in the most efficient manner, maintaining a sustainable environment etc.

We are unable to make full use of the knowledge that is generated. This also raises the question whether what we acquire is relevant knowledge to improve our quality of life or harmful knowledge that adversely affects the quality of life.

Crimes of various types are on the increase. Values, which maintained the relationships in society, are declining and disappearing. We have so many specialized courses and programs of education. But they seek to improve the material advancement of man. They provide career opportunities. But they draw blank when coming to character formation, which is a major indication of man's real progress and quality of life. Have we made any progress in improving the character of man? This task is left to religious and spiritual organizations. Is not character formation an ingredient of economic development?

Progress can be sustained only if any program implemented is rooted in human character. This means a well disciplined code of conduct self imposed by the individual for the best contribution from him and for the good of society.

The ingredients of quality of life are: pollution free environment, harmonious relations within communities, decline in crime, value based leadership, a feeling of safety, absence of fear, positive roles for government, institutions, citizens, maintenance of law and order, sifting relevant knowledge and rejecting irrelevant knowledge, absence of discrimination among people positive role of media, press, films, books and substituting the philosophy of glorification of crime and immorality by that of glorification of character, contribution and social harmony.

There is dethronement of wisdom. The great and cherished treasured values are thrown to the winds by a vast majority of the population who live a life at the level of the senses. We say civilization has advanced.

Are we making any serious effort to reverse the trend except crying from roof tops that the scourge of terrorism and vice afflicts the world? Is it not time to wake up and act? We realize that cancer caused by tobacco use or smoking is an evil and treatment of this disease costs more than the revenue earned from tobacco products. Why not we realize that lack of character in humans is the chronic disease.

To reverse the trend and reduce the intensity of the damage caused why not give priority to character formation and development in all our learning and research methodologies? Why not incorporate this as an essential ingredient of progress in all branches of knowledge. There is no dearth of resources for reversing the adverse trend. Words of ancient wisdom are contained in the scriptures of all religions. We have to dig out and use them liberally. The curative properties of these works are great and marvelous and have been proved by the test of time.

Texts like the Bhagavad-Gita contain enormous potential for the benefit of mankind. It focuses only on the positive aspects and the good of man. It is a tool of motivation and human excellence. It has relevance to nation building and character and leadership development. Only men of character and vision in any field of activity, be it science, economics or politics, alone can deliver the goods on a lasting basis and ensure global prosperity and harmony. They will be anchored in spirituality. Only then we will have real progress with global harmony and happiness.

The human mind has to set its direction towards achieving this goal. It does not matter if it takes time. But the progress achieved will be lasting and solid. Otherwise we will produce more and more Nobel laureates but also a cluster of sick societies where man is preoccupied only with selfish interests, leaving the poor to their fate from which relief is almost impossible for them for decades.

This calls for the best of management of the human faculties at the individual level. It is self-management. It means rectifying the imbalance in the body, mind and intellect function. It will richly draw on the reservoir of talent and energy from inside, the God given internal resources, effectively for the benefit of society. Wisdom cannot be told. It has to be acquired through reflections on experience. This has to be done through mind control, positive thinking, and a healthy body.

We must stretch our minds to the farthest limit; take care of the body through yogic exercises, proper breathing and control of food. Yoga postures with proper breathing will ensure stamina, efficiency and good health. By living in the present we can manage time better. We can attain excellence by adding to our work age-old time-tested values. Spiritual strength that comes from the faith in a supreme power above man is the greatest asset. Man benefits by developing and holding on to it. We gain considerably if every field of human activity brings value systems in its fold.